the most comfortable sock in the world!

T25

OUR DJ
Photographs by D J McNeill

Down Survey 2007

Yearbook of Down County Museum

Editor: M Lesley Simpson

Published by Down County Museum

OUR DJ

Photographs by D J McNeill

Down Survey 2007

Yearbook of Down County Museum

Editor: M Lesley Simpson

Photograph credits:
All images printed by Allen Thompson, ABIPP, from photographs taken by D J McNeill, except for Plate 1.9 and photograph of D J McNeill's cameras, both by Allen Thompson.

ISBN 978-0-9532530-9-8

The publication of this volume was generously supported by the Friends of Down County Museum. Members of the Friends will receive a free copy. Membership information is available from the museum at
The Mall, Downpatrick, County Down, BT30 6AH

Telephone: 028 44 61 5218 **Fax:** 028 44 61 5590 **Email:** museum@downdc.gov.uk

Designed and printed by: TSO Ireland

Front cover picture:
This photograph of a bicycle for three is a good example of D J McNeill's opportunism. This was taken in 1954, in Newcastle.
05/73/160

Back cover picture:
The *Ben Varrey* aground at the mouth of Dundrum Bay in 1960.
05/49/61/01

CONTENTS

Some of D J McNeill's cameras, details in Appendix.

FOREWORD

The photographic archive is one of the most important parts of the Down County Museum collection. Spanning the years from the later 19th century to the present day, it provides a significant resource for anyone studying the history of County Down. The images have proved invaluable for incorporating in our exhibitions and we have already published a number in previous issues of the Down Survey [1]. Other individuals and organisations have also been able to make good use of photographs from this archive.

During the course of this year work has begun on a major, long term project to improve the storage of the photographs. Some types of photographic negative are notoriously unstable so proper conservation and storage is required to ensure future access. At the same time we have been updating files and editing indexes. This work was largely undertaken by volunteers Sharon and Noel Hogg and Victoria Newberry.

The purpose of this publication is to record, in a permanent form, a selection from the archive and is another step forward in making our collection more accessible. This volume is dedicated to photographs taken by D J McNeill. While it can only be a very small sample of the many thousands of photographs which he took in his lifetime, it nevertheless gives some idea of the extent of his interest, his enthusiasm and opportunism.

However, the book would not have been possible without the help of many people. The text and captions were written by museum staff, with help from the McNeill family and members of the community. For the last twenty years the museum has been fortunate in having a photographer as experienced as Allen Thompson on our staff. His skills were vital in the selection and printing of images for this book. We are very grateful to Gerard Lennon, formerly Community Education Officer at the museum, Spencer Cusack of Downpatrick, Brownlow McClean of Dundrum and Tom Walsh of Newcastle for their assistance. A special debt of gratitude is owed to Elizabeth and Frances McNeill who provided background information about images as well as support in general for the work of the museum. We hope this book will be a fitting memorial to their father.

M Lesley Simpson
Keeper of Collections
2007

1

Daniel J McNeill at Murlough House, Dundrum.
05/49/182/01

1. D J MCNEILL

Daniel Joseph McNeill, or 'DJ' as he was widely known, was born in Dundrum in 1906. He was educated at the local primary school and at Hughes Academy, Belfast. His teaching career began at St Malachy's College, and the Christian Brothers School, in Belfast, in the 1930s. He moved to Further Education, first at Stranmillis College, then Bangor, before coming to Downpatrick in 1944, where he spent the rest of his working life.

He married Mollie Fitzpatrick in 1937, and his three children, Dan, Elizabeth and Frances were born in 1940, 1942 and 1949. The family retained their close links with their Flynn and McNeill relations in Dromara and Dundrum, as can be seen in many photographs. Mollie died in 1983 and sadly, young Dan himself died in 1992.

DJ was totally involved in the community and was a member of many local organisations. These included the Downpatrick Hospital Management Committee, Quoile Yacht Club, Dundrum Regatta and Sports Committee, Lecale Historical Society, the local Young Farmers Club, Downpatrick Golf Club, the Downe Society, Patrician Youth Club, Portaferry Camera Club, Newcastle Field Club, the Downpatrick and Ardglass Railway Society and the 'Woodbutchers'. He was also a member of the Institute of British Architects, a President of the Principals of Technical Schools in Northern Ireland and was on the board of the City and Guilds Examiners. As a result, he was widely respected as a teacher, administrator and historian. In 1966 he was awarded the MBE for his contribution to Technical Education and in 1986 the local community recognised his work by giving him the Down District Visual Arts Award.

He began taking photographs in his teens. The earliest in our archive were taken with a Box Brownie camera, bought from Mr Smiley, the chemist in Castlewellan, for 15s 6d, in June 1922 when he was only fifteen. Unfortunately these images have deteriorated so cannot be included here. From this beginning he went on to publish photographs regularly in newspapers, the first in the *Irish News* in 1947 and later in the *Mourne Observer, Northern Whig, North Down Chronicle* and *Bangor Spectator*. He began a life-long association with the *Down Recorder* in 1951 and contributed to local journals and magazines. In 1960, DJ was commissioned by the British Museum to take photographs of Killyleagh and the surrounding area for an exhibition about Hans Sloane. Throughout his adult life he took his camera everywhere and has left us an unparalleled record of life in our county from the 1940s to the 1980s. But he also copied old photographs which people brought to him. From these sources he created lively slide shows, which many people remember with affection.

From its inception DJ supported this museum, inspiring and encouraging staff and he was unfailingly generous with his time, information and photographs. After his death in 1988, DJ's family gave to the museum his entire collection of photographs, along with other items listed in the Appendix. Many local people have helped us to sort and index the negatives. We have since printed selections of the photographs for exhibition as well as using some for postcards and greetings cards. However, we have always intended to produce a more permanent record of the collection. We hope other books will follow this one.

1.2 Four generations

D J McNeill with his father James, his son Dan and grandmother Elizabeth Flynn, neé Branagh, photographed September 1940.
05/43/01/02

1.3 Theresa Fitzpatrick and Dan McNeill

DJ photographed his sister-in-law, Theresa Fitzpatrick, with Dan, on a visit to Scrabo Tower, Newtownards about 1942.
05/79/02/01

6

1.4 Dan and Elizabeth McNeill

The children were photographed at Clonachullion, near Bryansford, about 1948.
05/75/31/01

1.6 Elizabeth McNeill

Elizabeth feeding her pet lamb at her Granny Flynn's farm in Upper
Crossgare, Dromara, 1952.
05/43/01/03

1.7 St John's Point

Elizabeth McNeill
photographed at St John's
Point lighthouse, about 1955
05/62/01/01

1.8 The 'Forty Flynns'

The Flynn family were photographed at a family gathering at the Flynn farm in 1959. There are too many people to name here but all the details have been recorded by the family [2].
05/43/01/04

1.9 Preview of exhibition of D J McNeill's photographs at Down County Museum

The first exhibition of DJ's photographs 'Our DJ' opened in 1991. From left to right are Dr Brian Turner, Curator, and later Director, of Down County Museum (1981-1999), Elizabeth, Frances and Dan McNeill.

2. DUNDRUM

My work is the embodiment of dreams
William Morris, philosopher and influential designer, 1856.

These words could be used to describe the camera work of D J McNeill, whose close attachment to the village and people of Dundrum has been amply demonstrated by the photographs taken there by him over many decades. He guaranteed authentic pictures of those enduring faces and places by the exuberance of his nature and that informal and friendly approach to all his subjects.

D J McNeill's parents, James McNeill and Mary Flynn, were originally both from Dromara but his father became a partner in the building firm of Flynn and McNeill, based in Dundrum. It was here that DJ was born and brought up. Although his work later took him elsewhere, he often returned, and always with his camera.

The highlight of the year was the annual Regatta and Sports and DJ was its chairman for nearly twenty years. However, his photographs covered numerous events beyond this, such as musicals, confirmations, school activities, gymkhanas, family groups, local characters and buildings which have now gone or been altered beyond recognition. The railway and harbour activities were special to him as they involved people and technology and he enjoyed being there in the bustle of everyday life.

These images are only a fragment of DJ's output but they are an appropriate reflection of his enduring pride in the village and village life.

2.1 View of Dundrum and the Mournes

This view, with the Mournes in the background, was taken before the new road was built in the 1970s. The town itself had been 'improved' by Lord Downshire in the mid nineteenth century. This work included the construction of a new pier, warehouses, bathhouses, inn and houses. 05/49/148/01

2.2 Dundrum Bay

Photographed in 1969, this view through the Bar to the Irish Sea was taken from the ramparts of the castle. It demonstrates why the site was chosen by John de Courcy in the twelfth century. The castle occupies a prominent position with views of the surrounding land and has access to a good natural harbour. The town probably began to develop in medieval times to service the castle, although not on the same scale as Carrickfergus, which also grew up around a castle founded by de Courcy.
05/49/168/01

FLYNN&McNEILL
BUILDERS&CONTRACTORS
PHONE
11
DUNDRUM.

2.4 Gymkhana committee

The Gymkhana was held at Moneylane in 1944. Members of the committee are, on the back row from left to right : Kathleen McKeating, Rosaline McMullan, Ruby Coulter, Josephine Magee, Sadie Trohear, Bella Grant, Annie McCavery, Eileen Deeny, Nan Hughes, Maggie Glavin, Margaret McClune, -?
Front row, left to right: Jane Maitland, Rosalind Black, W McMullan, S Campbell, Elizabeth Imrie, Letitia Flynn, W Bates, Nancy McClean, Norah Fitzpatrick, Nessie McKinney, Beannie McSpadden.
Food rationing was still in progress and the 'banana' sandwiches were made from boiled parsnips, grated and mixed with banana essence!
05/49/106/01

2.5 Gymkhana at Murlough Farm

The man on the right is Whitfield Thompson, photographed in 1951.
05/49/107/01

2.8 On the battery

Seen here during the Regatta in 1957 are John McKeating senior, Peter Savage, James McClune, Eddie Flynn, William Glavin, John McKinney senior, Charles Mitchell, Brownlow McClean, William Crone (the East Downshire manager), Danny Flynn, Sam McCall, Eddie McClean, William McMurray and William Ogle. In the background can be seen a dredger, buoys and coal bucket.
05/49/14/01

Becalmed at the start! This shows a handicap race, about 1958, involving Flying Fifteens and Lightnings. The starting line, from battery to buoy, was also the finishing line after the boats had completed the prescribed course over the inner bay. Ballykinler beach is in the background and Redmond's Point just out of view on the left.
05/49/14/02

2.10 Fancy dress parade

The participants are parading down Main Street during the Regatta and Sports in 1959. The officials were, from left to right, Thomas McClean, Danny Flynn, William McMurray, Peter Savage, John McKinney and John Keating. The horse rider is Hugh McKay. Frances McNeill was in the parade, dressed as Red Riding Hood.
05/49/04/02

2.11 Swimmers

These young men raced across the harbour to Redmond's Point and back, about 1962. Back row, left to right: Danny Flynn, Peader Savage, Pat McKeating, Eamon Flynn, Jerome Flynn, Elias Connor, and Eddie Flynn. Front row, from left to right: Malachy Glavin, Thomas Kilmartin, Eddie McKay, Sean Flynn and Pachal Flynn.
05/49/34/01

2.14 The *Ben Varrey*

This ship, bringing coal from Liverpool to Dundrum, ran aground
at the mouth of Dundrum Bay in 1960.
05/49/61/01

2.15 The *MV Gloria*

Photographed about 1968, the cargo on the quay includes pit props
for coal mines. Timber was brought from Tollymore and other local
forests to Dundrum. From here it was transported to the Bristol
Channel and Wales.
05/49/62/01

2.16 The *SS Downshire*

After the closure of the rail link, the East Downshire Steamship
Company transported coal from the port by lorry fleet. Note the
trolley system to the shed over the lorry on the right. Coal was the
only product passing through the port in later years but at one time
Dundrum had been a very busy port with grain, stone from local

2.17 Removal of coal

Alex Connor is guiding the crane driver of the grab system for the removal of coal from the boat. This system was used until the port was closed in 1984. The last cargo went out on 31 March that year and the navigation lights were removed in the summer.
05/49/67/01

2.18 Clearing up coal

Charles Taylor and Paddy Brady are clearing up on the 'ceiling' of a coal boat after the grab clearance, 1974. The driver is Billy Heenan. 05/49/67/02

2.19 and 2.20 The Castle Vaults public house

This public house was originally built about 1890 for John McClafferty who came from Donegal. DJ photographed the building on Main Street in 1935, and after it was extensively damaged by a bomb in 1972.
05/49/133/01 and 05/49/133/02

2.22 Annie Simons

Annie feeding swans at Keel Point, 1966.
05/49/183/01

2.23 The Kielty family

Photographed in 1983 are Patrick, Cahal, John senior, Ned and John Junior. The road race, covering eight miles, was part of the Regatta programme.
05/49/393

2.24 P E Display

Gymnastics was just one of the activities of an efficiently organised Youth Club. It was directed by Danny Flynn, Principal of the Sacred Heart School and a highly qualified P E instructor. This tableau was part of a display for parents, friends and villagers in the Aquinas Hall, newly erected when this photograph was taken about 1952. Second from the left is Terry Caldwell and at the centre lying on the ground is Tommy McShane. At the back, left of centre, on a boy's shoulders, is Ed McKeating and to the right of the centre Tony Kilmartin is sitting on the shoulders of Pascal Flynn.
05/49/453/01

2.25 Dundrum Dramatic Society

Photographed in 1957 are, standing left to right: Paschal Flynn,
Fr Darragh, Noel Flynn, Jerome Flynn, Thomas Forsythe, Sean Flynn,
Fr Gogarty PP and Patrick McClean. Seated : Lizzie McPoland,
Bernadette Glavin and Imelda Glavin.
05/49/191/01

3. DOWNPATRICK

The economic fortunes of Downpatrick [3] have gone up and down from the time when it was first chosen as a strategic site in medieval times. The town was at a low ebb in the sixteenth century, reached its peak in the eighteenth and nineteenth centuries and then went into a slow decline until relatively recently. Downpatrick has been fortunate in its chroniclers and recorders. From the late eighteenth century Aynsworth Pilson's diary gives us an evocative picture of a changing town. Earlier maps and paintings give us some idea of the layout of the town and of improvements being made. However, it is from the later nineteenth century that we begin to get a more accurate picture of what Downpatrick actually looked like through the widespread use of photography to record buildings and streets. For the first time we also get an impression of the dress and appearance of many ordinary people. One of the most important chroniclers of the mid twentieth century was D J McNeill, whose collection of photographs of the town add immeasurably to the historic record.

This section of DJ's photographs includes some of the most significant images in the archive, recording major demolition and reconstruction of buildings which took place in Downpatrick in the 1960s and 1970s. There must have been times during this period when much of the town was like a building site. Whole streets were replaced and new housing estates built on the outskirts of the town. The impetus for the replacement of old housing stock was the poor living conditions endured by many people in the town. The County Council and Urban District Council were anxious to improve standards of housing and ensure that townspeople had access to more modern facilities. Some of DJ's photographs show just how bad some of the housing was but in the drive to demolish sub standard dwellings many significant eighteenth and nineteenth century buildings, which should have been preserved, were lost. As well as housing local people, the local authorities also had to respond to the need to house many people arriving in Downpatrick following the widespread violence in Belfast in the late 1960s and early 1970s. DJ recorded the construction of new estates at the Flying Horse and Model Farm which housed many of these new settlers to the town. As DJ took or collected photographs to show both the old and the new, we can now compare and contrast the town before and after the widespread changes of these years.

The daily lives of Downpatrick people and social change, after the Second World War, are also represented here. The closure of the railway and gas works reflects both technological developments and political decisions. The photographs taken by DJ to record these events are very poignant, showing the demise of enterprises central to a county town's sense of importance in the mid twentieth century. At the same time that some traditional features of the town were in decline, education obviously wasn't as the many shots of schools opening or being expanded show. DJ was on hand to record the establishment of all these new educational initiatives. On a lighter note, events such as the Canon's Excursion to Newcastle remind us of an era when more innocent pastimes held sway and children were thrilled at the prospect of a day's entertainment by the seaside! As well as conveying a strong feeling of community and identity these photographs provide one of the most valuable resources we have to reconstruct the recent past of this most historic town.

3.1 Bridge Street

This view from Bridge Street, taken about 1970 after some of the old houses had been demolished, shows eighteenth and nineteenth century buildings along with some of the newly built housing stock. The new Fountain Street flats (now demolished) can be seen in the far background. In the 1960s and 1970s local authorities throughout Europe regarded high rise housing stock and flats as the way forward. From the late 1980s and 1990s this view was challenged with 'traditional' housing seen as being a better way to promote community values. Nowadays the shortage of land for housing has seen a revival of flats although now they are usually called apartments!

3.2 Bridge Street

This view shows a former public house in Bridge Street, 1967. Posing for the camera are members of the Rea family, from left to right, Lesley, Valerie, Kenneth and Desmond. Although the houses in this area badly needed to be replaced the residents were unhappy with the maisonettes they were being offered. The council eventually agreed to build them proper houses.
05/42/13

3.3 and 3.4 Bridge Street

These two images are a good example of how D J McNeill recorded
the development of the town, before and after building took place.
The local building firm of H J O'Boyle was responsible for work here
as elsewhere in the town.
05/42/01/01 and 05/42/20/01

3.5 Church Street

The building on the corner of Church Street and English Street, was formerly the Post Office. It was purchased by the Down Recorder in 1964 and the newspaper has been produced there since. The *Downpatrick Recorder* was founded by Conway Pilson in 1836 and for many years was printed in premises on Irish Street. Tradition says the old Post Office was on the site of Castle Dorras, the town's medieval gaol. The old gas lamp has been re-used as a sign post. 05/42/77/01

3.6 Church Street

D J McNeill took this photograph of crowds standing outside Charlie Thompson's 'Black and White' Garage watching the first television for sale in Downpatrick, probably in the early 1950s. A Mr Mees bought this garage in 1956/57 from Charlie Thompson. The Mees also owned two petrol stations in the town, one on Church Street. Mr Mees sold bicycles, motorcycles, cars and radios from this shop. His son Charles remembers similar gatherings outside the later shop to view the newest motorcycle or bike.
05/42/72/01

3.7 Church Street

Hugh Mullan, chimney sweep,
photographed in 1974.
05/42/117

3.8 Edward Street

This photograph records the opening and blessing of the new De La Salle Boys' Intermediate Secondary School which officially opened in 1953. The man with the glasses is the architect, Thomas McClean who is handing the keys of the building to Bishop Magean. Left to right are Fr F G McNamara C C, Fr Neil McCamphill C C, Bishop Magean and Fr Patrick Maginn C C.
05/40/06/01

3.9 English Street

This Georgian house was demolished about 1955. English Street and Stream Street still retain some significant Georgian buildings.
05/41/677/01

3.10 English Street

Crowds gather to watch the South Staffordshire Regiment on parade opposite the Courthouse on the first morning of the quarterly Assize Court, about 1950.
05/41/1002

3.11 and 3.12 Fountain Street

This part of the town has been radically changed as can be seen from the before and after views.
05/40/21/01 and 05/40/22/01

3.14 Irish Street

Canon McWilliam's excursion to Newcastle was organised annually in the summer, until 1970. The excursion began in 1928 and initially took place to Killough. Newcastle became the regular destination from 1933 onwards. A local committee collected money to take about 1500 children from local primary and secondary schools to the seaside for the day, in the early years by train and after 1950 by bus. The excursion took place in June and St Catherine's Band from Newry traditionally led the procession from Edward Street and Mary Street, down Irish Street to Market Street. Other bands included the Annacloy Accordian Band, Erenagh Pipe Band, Magheralagan Pipe Band and St Peter's Band from Belfast. Children who had made their First Holy Communion in the preceding May usually walked directly after the first band. This photograph, probably taken about 1968 or 1969, shows St Patrick's Band, Downpatrick, bringing up the end of the procession. The leader of the band is Tom Rea. Behind him left is Mel McGrady, centre is John Kelly and right Tommy McLoughlin.
05/40/98/01

3.15 John Street

After it had gone out of use as a school the building was used as a men's club, for meeting or playing billiards.
05/40/161/01

3.16 John Street

People came from far and wide to attend the Sunday night dances held in the Canon's Hall, with bands such as the Pioneers and Melody Aces providing the entertainment. The building was demolished in 1980. Today, the Patrician Youth Centre stands on this site.
05/40/149/01

3.18 Market Street

This view shows the Railway Station about 1950, shortly before it closed. The line had opened about a hundred years before. The two cars parked at the front are taxis run by the Connollys. Although the station was demolished, trains are now running again as a visitor attraction at the Railway Museum.
05/41/1003/01

3.19 Market Street

The spring thaw in 1963 caused severe flooding in the town. Although that year was worse than usual, the town flooded regularly until the Quoile barrage scheme was completed.
'The floods are up in Market Street
The station's on the shore
And Paddy Kelly's glad to hear
It ain't gonna rain no more'
Paddy Kelly was a publican with premises on Market Street.
05/4/1004/01

3.20 Market Street

The old town Gas Works opened in 1848 and closed in 1959.
05/41/356/01

3.21 Market Street

This view shows the Gas Manager's house (now reconstructed across
the road as the Railway Station for the Railway Museum).

3.22 Market Street

The owner of the Gas Works, Bernard (Barney) Morgan, is putting the
last shovel of coal into the retorts in 1958, prior to closing.
05/41/356/03

3.23 Market Street

Cattle are grazing on Fair Green in 1954, after being graded and sold in the adjacent market yards and before being sent to the abattoir on Irish Street. This field was to become the site of the new Technical College.
05/41/312

3.25 and 3.26 St Patrick's Avenue

New shops and a garage replaced the old cottages on the corner of St Patrick's Avenue. The old photograph also shows the gate lodge for the Downe Hospital. In about 1940 the families living in these two-room houses included the Graceys, the Perrys, Ma Walsh, the McDowells, the McVeighs and Johnny Fitzsimons.
05/41/439/01 and 05/41/439/02

3.27 St Patrick's Avenue

There was a double celebration being recorded in this photograph taken in 1955 outside St Patrick's Church. It was the centenary of the Sisters of Mercy arriving in Downpatrick as well as the Jubilee of Canon McWilliams. The Sisters of Mercy came to Downpatrick to provide education for both boys and girls and today the Convent of Mercy continues to provide primary education for girls. Part of the Sisters' original role was to educate poorer children. In the late nineteenth century they helped to subsidise this by providing private lessons in the 'accomplishments' of drawing, painting, music, singing and French for middle class girls. A bill dating from 1912 is in the museum collection and details the lessons given to one such family.
05/41/998/01

3.29 Flying Horse Estate

This new estate was photographed by D J McNeill in 1975. The Flying Horse estate takes its name from an eighteenth century inn which was located in this area. The nearby Model Farm estate is so called because of the 'model farm' which was intended to be established here by the will of Thomas Henry, but as far as is known, was never built.
05/41/834/01

4. AROUND THE COUNTY

D J McNeill took photographs wherever he went and many of those illustrated in this chapter demonstrate his opportunism in photographing whatever was happening at the time. The coverage is better for some towns than others; this merely reflects where his roots were and where he spent most time, whether through work or visiting friends and family. It is not an indication that he found any place uninteresting - he probably just hadn't been there for any length of time! Indeed as his archive demonstrates clearly it was quite the opposite and the overriding impression we have is of DJ's interest in and enthusiasm for everything.

4.1 Annalong harbour

A peaceful view of the harbour and old corn mill, about 1953.
05/02/08/01

4.4 Bangor

A recruitment campaign for the Air Training Corps during World War II.
05/15/11/01

4.5 and 4.6 Bangor

On the beach, early 1940s. Was this a competition for the best pebble design?
05/15/13/01 and 05/15/13/02

4.7 and 4.8 Crossgar

Alex Campbell and his wife Hanna, photographed at their home in 1961. Alex was still thatching his roof at the age of 84.
05/35/35/01 and
05/35/35/02

4.9 Inch, near Downpatrick

Pupils and teachers at the primary school were photographed in 1960.
Their names have been recorded[4].
05/42/303

4.10 Kilkeel

The harbour was improved on several occasions, most recently in 1972.
05/60/13

This was taken looking from the Square up Newry Street and shows the traditional gathering place at the steps, 1954. The prominent Georgian building, with a facade of coursed granite blocks, dates from 1790.
05/60/01

4.12 Kilkeel

Market day, 1955.
05/60/04/01

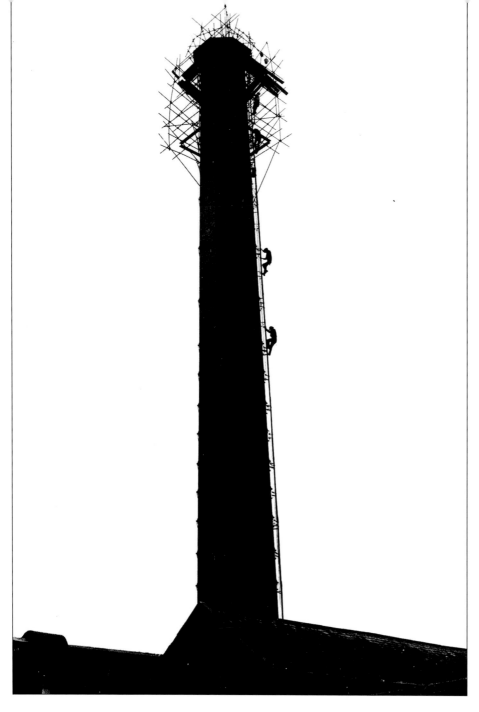

4.13 Killyleagh

Steeplejacks are working on the chimney at Shrigley Flax Spinning Mill, about 1960. Whilst dismantling part of the chimney, they narrowly escaped injury when some coping became dislodged, crashing into the mill below. 05/36/01/01

4.16 The Mournes

Men laying the road to the new waterworks, 1955.
05/89/08/01

4.17 Newcastle

The Percy French memorial fountain, removed since the photograph was taken. This commemorated Percy French, entertainer (1854-1920), who wrote the well-known song 'Where the Mountains of Mourne sweep down to the sea'.
05/73/94/01

4.18 Newcastle

Diver John McCallum prepares for work
laying sewer pipes for a new sewerage
scheme in 1955. On the left is Pat
McClelland, known locally as 'Footer' or
'Fig', Cox of the Newcastle lifeboat.
05/73/85/01

4.19 Newcastle

Sitting in the reserve lifeboat are Jimmy Smith, Assistant Mechanic and Sam McCullough, 2nd Cox. The man standing at the left may be Tony Course, Divisional Inspector, RNLI.
05/73/94/02

4.20 Newry

The town hall was built in 1893, to a design by William Batt. Here you can see it reflected in the still waters of the Clanrye River, in 1954. 05/74/04/01

4.21 The Newry Canal

The cargo ship *SS Dundalk* was a spectacular sight travelling on the canal from Newry to the Irish Sea, along the Newry to Omeath Road. One of the last maritime canals to be used in Ireland, it was closed shortly after this photograph was taken in 1959.
05/95/02/01

4.22 Newtownards

Photographed in 1953, the town hall was originally built as a market house in the 1760s to a design by Ferdinando Stratford, a Gloucestershire and Bristol bridge and river engineer. It is faced with local Scrabo sandstone.
05/79/03

4.23 Portaferry

The float competition is always a big event during Portaferry Gala.
'Noel's Ark' was photographed in 1977.
05/82/25/01

4.24 Portaferry

Drying dulse (seaweed), 1975. It was gathered from rocks at low tide
and dried for eating.
05/82/52/01

4.25 Portavogie

The photographer's brother John and a friend are inspecting work
at the harbour in 1953. The scheme cost £220,000 and by deepening
the harbour enabled fishing boats to enter and leave at any state of
the tide.
05/07/05/01

4.27 Warrenpoint

A pleasure boat is about to leave, probably for Carlingford. This was a popular excursion on a Sunday, especially before licensing laws changed in Northern Ireland.
05/92/04/01

5. THE TECHNICAL COLLEGE, DOWNPATRICK

The College was opened in November 1912 in a building on the corner of Bridge Street. The premises were structurally re-arranged and adapted at a cost of £120. In 1933 it moved to the site of the New Gaol in conjunction with the Down High School. When DJ succeeded Mr John McMeekin as Principal in 1944, the college had premises at various locations in the town, including the Old and New Gaols. He was largely responsible for its rapid development, always keen to introduce new subjects and courses, which resulted in a great increase in the number of students. But perhaps his most significant contribution was the transfer of the college to its present site on Market Street, which opened in September 1957. It was extended in 1966 but DJ also planned a further, major extension which was completed after his retirement.

During his time, eight outcentres were developed and improved for evening classes, at Ardglass, Clough, Glastry, Kircubbin and Portaferry, with new buildings at Crossgar, Killyleagh, and Portavogie. DJ sought to make maximum use of all the premises, catering for outside organisations wherever possible, except for political or religious purposes, thus ensuring the college was seen as serving the whole community. He was always quick to spot new trends and staff were encouraged to develop their ideas. In interviews he likened himself to the captain of a ship, steering from the bridge but always relying on the engine room crew, his staff, to keep the ship going. The good of the 'Tech' was always foremost in his mind. Although DJ retired in 1971 he remained part of college life and continued to teach woodwork to pupils of Down High School and Ardmore Special School.

The photographs in this section mirror the development of the College and the many events and changes in education which took place during DJ's time.

5.1 The old Technical School

This was the original building, opened in 1912, on the corner of Bridge Street.
48/02/524

5.2 Mr John McMeekin

He was Principal of the college from its foundation in 1912 to 1944. D J McNeill
photographed him in 1944 when he succeeded Mr McMeekin.
48/02/72

5.3 The new building

This opened on Fair Green, Market Street, in 1956. Here you can see staff, including James Ellis, P J Smyth, Hugh McNamara, Jim Curran and Harry Murtagh, and students posing on the site.
48/02/63/01

5.5 Opening of the Tuck Shop

Opened in the early 1980s this was greatly appreciated by both staff and students! Cutting the ribbon is Joe O'Riley, with Ken Lappin in the background. Queuing up are, second from right, Maureen Rice

5.6 Agriculture class in Downpatrick

Students are ploughing with horses on the Down High School site, 1955.
48/02/374/01

5.7 Agriculture class at Ballybeg

Students, with their teacher, P J Smyth of Annacloy in the centre, were photographed at James and Patrick Denvir's farm, 1955. They are making hay ropes and rolling them into balls or 'clews'. 05/03/70/01

5.10 Drama class

A performance of Macbeth took place at the Old Gaol (now the museum) in 1955.
48/02/114/01

5.11 Metalworking class

Students and their teacher in the metalworking shop.
48/02/329/01

This is one of the new courses started by DJ, in 1947-48. It became a popular course; here the teacher is Geoff Davidson.
48/02/645/01

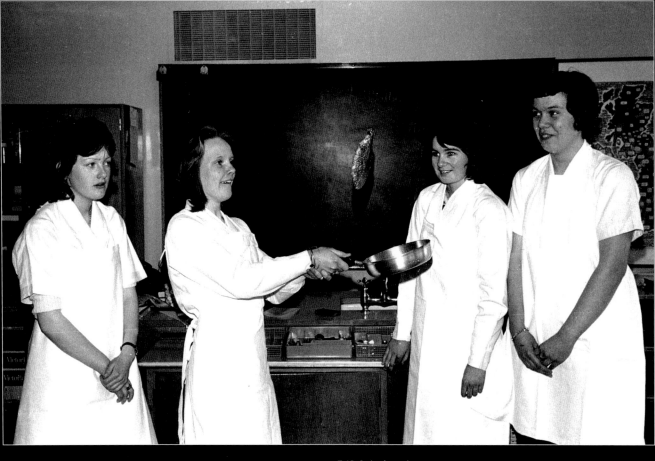

5.13 Catering class

Students tossing the pancake in March 1976.
48/02/285/01

5.14 Building class

Here students are constructing a scale bungalow in the garden of the Old Gaol (now the Museum), supervised by Edmund Patton, in 1978.
48/02/392/01

5.15 RSA student

Barbara Knox, student at the Ballynahinch campus, was awarded a bronze medal from the Royal Society of Arts for her outstanding results in the Stage II examination in Commercial Arithmetic. On the left is Willie Davidson, Chairman of the Board of Governors, and on the right James Ellis, Principal.
48/02/554/01

5.16 Computer class

The College leading the way with new courses in 1982. The teacher is
Kevin Ward.
48/02/534/01

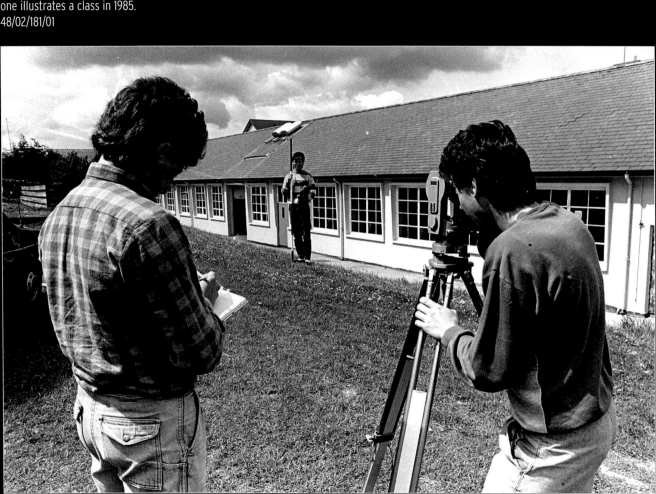

5.18 Textile students

Students on work experience at Killyleagh Spinning Mill, 1984.
48/02/673/01

5.19 Zebedee's Hat Shop

Students on work experience in the Rogers' family shop, Market
Street, Downpatrick, 1984.
48/02/669/01

5.21 Floral art display

5.22 Sports day

Sports Days were big events in the College calendar with students from all the colleges in County Down taking part. This high jump was photographed at Ballynahinch, 1983.
05/10/15/01

5.23 Football team

The team completed a marathon football match in 1974 which was
entered in the Guinness Book of Records.
48/02/132/01

6. WORK

Farming and fishing have been the mainstay of the economy in County Down for centuries and D J McNeill recorded both during his travels around the county. These images reflect the changing technology and economy during that time. When he first started taking photographs, ploughing with horses was still the norm. The photographs of fishing and associated work at Ardglass are a vivid reminder of this once thriving industry, as it was here and at other County Down ports such as Kilkeel and Portavogie.

There are still many small quarries in County Down but those extracting granite in the Mournes were formerly of major significance, exporting the stone to cities in Britain. Among the many changes which have taken place since then are those in working practices, such as health and safety!

6.1 Stackyard, Denvir's farm, Ballybeg, near Downpatrick.

Left to right are James Denvir, Patrick Denvir, John Telford and Alan Freeman, photographed in 1955.
05/03/69/01

6.2 Ploughing

At Moneybot, about 1956.
05/90/19/01

6.3 Reaper and binder

Cutting and binding at Gilmore's farm, Killyleagh, 1961.
05/63/27

The Corrigan brothers were photographed at Strangford, 1956.
05/90/121/01

6.5 Potato harvest

Stopping for tea at the Crea family farm, Grangewalls, near
Downpatrick. First left is Susan Crea, second from right Bert Crea.
05/62/06/01

6.6 Packing fish

D J McNeill recorded many aspects of the fishing industry at
Ardglass, of which the following are just a few. This one shows men
packing fish on the *Moravia*.
05/03/37/01

6.7 Women sorting fish

At Ardglass.
05/03/37/02

6.8 Mending nets

At Ardglass.
05/03/46/01

6.10 Barrels

Packed with fish and ready to be transported, at Ardglass.
05/03/46/03

6.11 Loading fish

From the harbour to lorries
at Ardglass, 1984.
05/03/8/04

6.12 Herring packers at Ardglass Quay

Women from Donegal worked with local people, packing herrings into barrels for export to Europe. Second from the right here is Mary Cochrane of Ardglass, photographed in 1950.
05/3/124/01

6.13 and 6.14 Stone working

Granite being unloaded and cut into blocks at Annalong.
05/02/08/02 and 05/02/08/03

6.15 Stone working

The stonemason finishes the granite blocks.
05/02/08/04

7. LEISURE AND SPORT

In this section you can see the varied and changing ways in which people enjoyed their leisure time, whether through organised sports or in family groups. After the Second World War most people worked shorter hours so had more free time. The towns of Bangor and Newcastle have a long history as holiday resorts, reflected in some of the images shown in this section. Before foreign travel became affordable for ordinary working people, a day at the seaside was something to look forward to. Some events, such as horse racing, have retained their interest and even increased in popularity, while going to the 'pictures' declined, with many local cinemas closing in the 1970s, before becoming fashionable once more at the end of the twentieth century. The GAA, especially after the success of the county team in the 1960s, provided popular outlets for the young men of the parish. The photographs show relatively few women taking part in sports. However, this may not be as true a reflection of sport in the mid twentieth century as the gender separation seen in education and work. Those photographs provide an important social comment.

TONIC

CINEMA BALLROOM CAFE

MARIO LORENZI · FOGEL & LADY
JOSEPH CALLEIA A MAN OF THE PEOPLE

MOIRA DRIVE

7.1 Bangor

7.2 Dundrum and Dromara Gaelic football teams

They were photographed at Moneylane, in 1952. The Dromara team are wearing striped socks and shirts. On the left is Parish Priest Fr Gogarty and on the right coach Danny Flynn.
05/41/192/01

7.3 Bryansford Players

Performing 'The Auction of Killybuck' in 1954 are, from left to right, Joe O'Kane, Jimmy McClements, Joe McClean, Peter McKinney, James McClarnon, Jimmy Campbell, Desmond Egan and James Agnew. The two ladies at the front are Ita Murray and Maureen Gammon. 05/75/22/01

7.4 Dog show

The Newcastle (County Down) and District Canine Society was founded in 1949 and held its first show in 1950. This show was photographed in 1954.
05/73/07/01

7.5 Cyclists in Newcastle

This photograph of a bicycle for three is a good example of
D J McNeill's opportunism. Mr and Mrs Robinson and their daughter
Joan, from Cregagh, Belfast, were photographed in 1954.
05/73/160

7.6 Mountain race

These men are setting off from outside the old Newcastle Urban District (known locally as the Municipal) Council offices, Newcastle, to climb Slieve Donard 1955. This event still takes place.
05/73/98/01

7.7 Downpatrick race course

Horse racing at the course on Ballydugan Road, 1955. Vere Essex
Cromwell established a course in Downpatrick, by royal patent, in 1685.
05/41/1000/01

7.10 Donkey and pony Derby

At Donard Park, Newcastle, 1959.
05/73/10/01

7.11 The Sam Maguire Cup

The All Ireland Gaelic Football trophy came to Down in 1960.
Photographed with it here are members of the Flynn family, along
with the National League Cup and the St Brendan Cup. The latter was
played for between winners of the All Ireland League and the New
York League. Standing at the back are Danny Flynn (second from
right) and DJ (fourth from right).
05/49/190/01

These four children were able to skate on the frozen water of the
marshes in Downpatrick during the severe winter of 1962-1963.
05/41/997

7.14 Horse show

Isobel McAuley of Bangor was photographed receiving the Challenge Cup from Mr A L Colgan. She was riding Kearney Joker, belonging to Patrick Morgan of Dooey, Portaferry in the Donkey Derby on the Annesley Estate at Castlewellan Castle, 1967.
05/26/19/01

7.15 Saintfield Show

Gary Meekin of Belfast, on his Russian-bred horse Reshim, is on his way to winning the Guinness Qualifying Competition at the show, 1967. 05/86/04/01

7.17 International ploughing match

At Patrick Forde's estate at Seaforde, 1978.
05/87/47/01

7.18 Regatta

Strangford, 1960. Windmill Hill, Portaferry can be seen in the
background.
05/90/27/01

7.19 Skittles match

This sponsored match took place at McLeigh's Bar, Ballynoe and was
in aid of the Day Centre. This summer game used to be played on
roads but is now organised as a bar league.
03/62/45

APPENDIX

The D J McNeill Collection

(Recorded in the museum register, DB281-2, 314-318, 335-342, 350-352, received between June 1988 and April 1989)

Photographs

B/W negatives (35mm and larger format)	approx 20,000
Colour negatives	approx 15,000
Glass plates (quarter and half plates)	approx 122
Lantern slides (B/W)	approx 830
Lantern slides (colour)	3 sets
Colour transparencies (35mm)	approx 2000
Files of photographic prints, newspaper cuttings and other information	approx 65

The B/W negatives and 35mm colour slides are indexed according to the museum system.

Cameras

Seven cameras:
Kodak No 2 Bulls Eye box camera for roll film.
DCM1993-30
Zeiss Ikon Contessa Nettel, folding bellows plate camera.
DCM1993-42
Zeiss Ikon Super Ikonta folding bellows camera for roll film.
DCM1993-83
Zeiss Ikon Super Ikonta folding bellows camera for roll film.
DCM1993-43
Kodak Retina IIIc folding couple rangefinder camera, 35mm.
DCM1993-16
Zenit B SLR camera, 35mm.
DCM1993-18
Hannimex 35S SLR camera, 35mm
DCM1993-17

DJ bought a German Super Ikonta in the 1930s (probably one of those listed above), and a Pentax ME Super in the 1970s. His favourite in the 1980s was a Minox 35GT [5].

Photographic accessories

'Optiscope' projector.
DCM2007-77
Spare lenses.
DCM1993-57, 59, 62
Filter.
DCM1993-60
Set of close-up tubes, 'Aico' and extension rings.
DCM1993-58 and 61
Slide duplicator, 'Panagor'.
DCM1993-63
Close-up rangefinder.
DCM1993-64
Stereoscopic slide viewer (plastic) and two rolls of stereoscopic film.
DCM2007-81 and 82
5 packets of unused film.
DCM2007-83
Box of carbon paper, used for typing on to slides.
DCM2007-84
Contact printing frames.
DCM2007-85
Print meter.
DCM2007-86

2 medals awarded to R D Perceval [6].
DCM1995-85 and 86

In addition to the above, a variety of other objects were received as part of this donation. They include books, archive material, a sundial, toys and household items. Further details available in the museum.

Girls from an orphanage

In addition to all the photographs which he took himself, DJ also copied many older photographs. This one, of girls from an orphanage in Downpatrick, is just one example from this part of the archive. While some of these images may have been published individually, as a group they are a significant resource. They could be the basis for another book!
05/40/138

REFERENCES

1. See especially 'Down through the Lens' by M Lesley Simpson and Allen Thompson in *Down Survey* 2001.

2. The names of the Flynn family are as follows:
   Back row: Monica Walsh, Aidan Campbell, Dan McNeill junior, James O'Hare, Stephen O'Hare, John McNeill, Danny Walsh, Paschal Flynn, John O'Hare, Donal Flynn, Dan Flynn, Maurice Walsh, Sean Walsh, Nicky Walsh, Sean Duggan.
   Second row from back: James Gerard Walsh, Gerry Cleland, Colette Flynn, Elizabeth McNeill, Patricia Flynn, Jerome Flynn, Henry Flynn, D J McNeill.
   Third row: Seamus Duggan, Johnny Duggan, Josephine Duggan, Philomena Cleland, Margaret Campbell, Thomas McShane, Peggy McShane, Eilish Walsh, Pauline Walsh, Mae Flynn, Ena Flynn, Mollie McNeill, Aveen Flynn, Philomena Flynn, Danny Flynn, Mary McShane, Tom McShane.
   Fourth row: James McIlroy, E J Flynn, Sister Clare Flynn, Father Henry Flynn, Dan Flynn, Sister Mary Helena Flynn, Margaret Kelly, Jimmy Flynn, Sister Rosaleen Flynn, Clara O'Hare, Johnny Flynn, John Flynn.
   Sitting on front row: Kieran Walsh, Oliver Walsh, Patrick Duggan, Marie Duggan, Elizabeth Flynn, Ann Flynn, Claire Flynn, Catriona Flynn, Frances McNeill, Phil Flynn, Mary Flynn, John McShane, Raymond Walsh, Claire Byrne.

3. R H Buchanan and A Wilson, *Downpatrick*, Irish Historical Town Atlas, no 8, Royal Irish Academy, 1997.

4. The pupils and teachers have been identified as follows:
   Back row: Master Davidson, John Gordon, Peggy Shields, Alex McClurg, Kathleen McKee, Billy Cooper, Vera Shields, Jim Newell, Margaret Foley, Tom Osborne, Gertie Osborne, John Cochrane, Miss Swain.
   In front of Master Davidson: Frank Parkinson, Austin Emmett.
   Middle row: Tom Cochrane, Jim Morrison, Doris Parkinson, Dorothy McClurg, Bert Osborne, Stanley Parkinson, Billy Cochrane, Leslie Emmett, Jack McKee, Eileen Calvert, Ruth McMurray, Alma McClurg
   Sitting on front row: Ann McKee, ? , Daphne Emmett, ? , Bobby Shields, Grace Calvert, Ella White, Brian Parkinson, ? , Ann Morrison, ?

5. Alice Fitzpatrick, *D J McNeill, an Irish photographer,* unpublished manuscript, 1987.

6. Catalogued in 'Down through the Lens' by M Lesley Simpson and Allen Thompson in *Down Survey* 2001